ANIMALS Are NOT Like US
PIGS

For a free color catalog describing Gareth Stevens Publishing's list of high-quality books and multimedia programs, call 1-800-542-2595 (USA) or 1-800-461-9120 (Canada). Gareth Stevens Publishing's Fax: (414) 225-0377. See our catalog, too, on the World Wide Web: gsinc.com

Library of Congress Cataloging-in-Publication Data

Meadows, Graham.
    Pigs / by Graham Meadows.
      p. cm. — (Animals are not like us)
    Includes bibliographical references and index.
    Summary: Describes the physical characteristics and behavior of pigs, pointing out ways in which they differ from people.
    ISBN 0-8368-2254-4 (lib. bdg.)
    1. Swine—Juvenile literature.   2. Swine—Physiology—Juvenile literature. [1. Pigs.] I. Title. II. Series: Meadows, Graham. Animals are not like us.
SF395.5.M435   1998
636.4—dc21   98-18762

North American edition first published in 1998 by
Gareth Stevens Publishing
1555 North RiverCenter Drive, Suite 201
Milwaukee, WI 53212 USA

Original edition published in 1998 by Scholastic New Zealand Limited, 21, Lady Ruby Drive, East Tamaki, New Zealand. Original © 1998 by Graham Meadows. End matter © 1998 by Gareth Stevens, Inc.

Printed in the United States of America

1 2 3 4 5 6 7 8 9 02 01 00 99 98

ANIMALS Are NOT Like US
PIGS

Graham Meadows

Gareth Stevens Publishing
MILWAUKEE

Pigs are not like us.

Pigs have four
legs, not two.

Their legs are
short and stubby.

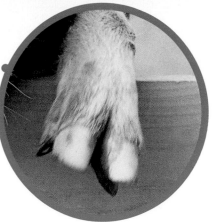

The hooves on the ends of their legs are called trotters.

Although their legs are short, pigs can run very fast.

Pigs have short, curly tails.

They can wag their tails, but not as fast as a dog can.

Pigs are not like us.

They don't wear clothes like we do.
Pigs have thick, hairy skin.

Some pigs have
pink skin.

Some pigs have
black skin.

Pigs keep their
skin healthy by
rolling in mud.

The mud helps
get rid of bothersome bugs.

Pigs are not like us.

They have more babies at one
time than humans do.

Female pigs are called sows.

They have up to sixteen babies at a time.

Their babies are called piglets.

Male pigs are called boars.

Pigs are not
like us.

They can't talk
like we do.

Pigs grunt
when they talk
to each other.

When they are angry, pigs bark like dogs.

When they are frightened, pigs squeal very loudly.

Pigs are not like us.

Their ears are different from ours.

Pigs' ears are big and floppy.

They can hear very well.

Pigs flap their ears to keep cool in hot weather.

Pigs are not like us.

They cannot see as well as we can.

Pigs have small eyes, but they know where to look for food.

Pigs are not like us.

They have much bigger noses than we do.

Pigs use their noses to dig in the ground for food.

16

Pigs like to
eat the roots
of plants.

They plow up the soil
and make quite a mess.

Pigs are not like us.

But sometimes we can
be just as messy!

Glossary

angry — feeling or showing unhappiness toward someone or something. *Cats hiss and raise their fur, and pigs may bark when they are **angry**.*

bark — the short, sharp sound made by dogs and some other animals. *Like dogs, pigs may **bark** when they are angry.*

boars — male pigs. ***Boars** mate with sows that then give birth to piglets.*

bothersome — disturbing or irritating. *Pigs sometimes roll in mud to get rid of **bothersome** bugs.*

different — not the same. *There are many **different** types of pigs.*

flap — to move the wings, arms, or another part of the body up and down. *Pigs do not have sweat glands, so they must **flap** their ears to keep cool during hot weather.*

floppy — not stiff or standing up straight; able to flop. *Pigs and some other animals have **floppy** ears.*

frightened — afraid of something or someone; scared. *A pig might make a squealing noise if it is **frightened**.*

grunt — a short, deep sound made by animals or people. *Pigs **grunt** as a way of communicating, or talking, with each other.*

hooves — the feet of animals, such as pigs, that have a tough, protective covering. *Besides pigs, cows, deer, and horses are other kinds of animals that have **hooves**.*

loudly — done with a loud noise. *Pigs may squeal* **loudly** *with a high tone when they are frightened.*

messy — not neat; untidy; dirty. *Some people think pigs are* **messy***, but pigs are actually very clean animals.*

piglets — baby pigs. *The mother pig, called a sow, can have up to sixteen* **piglets** *at a time, twice a year.*

plow — to break apart and turn over soil. *Humans* **plow** *the soil in a field with machines or with horses. Pigs* **plow** *the soil in the barnyard by pushing it with their noses.*

root — the part of a plant that usually grows down into the ground. It takes in water and minerals from the soil. The root of a plant also stores food and holds the plant in place. *Pigs like to eat the* **roots** *of some plants.*

soil — the loose top layer of dirt on the ground. *Pigs like to dig in the* **soil** *with their noses for food.*

sows — female pigs. *Sows carry their young for about 114 days.*

squeal — a high, loud sound or cry. *A pig may* **squeal** *when it is afraid.*

stubby — short and thick. *The legs of a pig are* **stubby***.*

trotters — the hooves on the ends of pigs' legs. *Pigs can run very fast on their hooved feet, or* **trotters***.*

wag — to move, swing, or wave something back and forth or up and down. *Some animals, including pigs and dogs,* **wag** *their tails when they are excited or happy.*

Activities

· ·

Make a Piggy Bank

To make your own piggy bank, wash and dry a half-gallon-size plastic milk jug. Turn it on its side and draw a slit at the top that is big enough for coins to fit through. Have an adult cut out the slit with a knife. With colorful markers, add details, such as eyes and a nose, to the "piggy." Glue on pieces of felt or colored paper for ears. Your piggy bank will sit firmly in place after the bottom gets heavy with the coins you save.

Barnyard Charades

This book shows some of the ways that pigs are *not* like us. It can be fun to play a game of barnyard charades and see if your friends and family can guess the animals you are imitating — by acting *like* these animals.

All in the Family

Female pigs are sows, male pigs are boars, and baby pigs are piglets. Make a list of several farm animals and see if you can think of the correct names for everyone in the "family." For example, female cattle are cows, male cattle are bulls, and baby cattle are calves.

Tails, You Win

Pigs are well known for their short, curly tails. The tails of various animals come in many different shapes and sizes. At your library, find a book on animals. Look at the pictures in the book, paying attention to the animals' tails. Can you find some that are short and curly, like a pig's? Look for the longest, the shortest, and other "winning" tails.

Books

Baby Pig. P. Mignon Hinds (Childrens Press Choice)

Curly, the Piglet. Cynthia Overbeck Bix (Carolrhoda)

Farm Animals. Animals at a Glance (series). Isabella Dudek (Gareth Stevens)

Farm Babies. Russell Freedman (Holiday House)

A Picture Book of Farm Animals. Mary Scott (Troll)

Pigs. Peter Brady (Bridgestone Books)

Pigs in the House. Steven Kroll (Gareth Stevens)

Pigs and Peccaries. Animal Families (series). Annemarie Schmidt and Christian R. Schmidt (Gareth Stevens)

Six Perfectly Different Pigs. Adrienne Geoghegan (Gareth Stevens)

Videos

Babe. (MCA Universal)

Barnyard Babies. (Video-11)

Charlotte's Web. (Paramount Home Video)

Farm Animals. (Good Apple)

Farm Animals and Their Mothers. (Phoenix/BFA)

Gordy. (Walt Disney Home Video)

The Pig. (Barr Films)

Pigs! (Churchill Media)

Pigs by Robert Munsch. (Golden Book Video)

Web Sites

homepages.ihug.co.nz/~ meadows/animal.htm

www.nppc.org/ForKids/farm tastic.html

Some web sites stay current longer than others. For further web sites, use your search engines to locate the following topics: *farm animals, farms, hogs, pigs,* and *swine.*

Index

Former veterinarian Graham Meadows is the author and/or photographer of over seventy books for children about animals.

It was while working as a vet at the Aukland Zoo in New Zealand that Graham Meadows's interest in animal photography began. He finds the way animals look and behave endlessly fascinating. His desire to pass on this enthusiasm to a younger generation has led him to produce the *Animals are not like us* series for three- to seven-year-olds.